A Girl's Guide to the

MARTIAL ARTS

Learn to practice basic poses in **Kung Fu, Karate, Tae Kwon Do, Jujitsu, Aikido,** and **Tai Chi Chuan**

Alice Jablonsky

Illustrations by
Shelly Meridith Delice

BARRON'S

MARTIAL ARTS

First edition for North America published in 2004
by Barron's Educational Series, Inc.

Created and produced by Orange Avenue Publishing, San Francisco, CA
© 2004 by Orange Avenue Publishing
Illustrations © 2004 by Shelly Meridith Delice

All inquiries should be addressed to:
Barron's Educational Series, Inc.
250 Wireless Boulevard
Hauppauge, NY 11788
http://www.barronseduc.com

Library of Congress Catalog Card No. 2003113643
International Standard Book No. 0-7641-2841-8

Printed in China
9 8 7 6 5 4 3 2 1

CREDITS

Creative Directors
Tanya Napier and Hallie Warshaw

Writer
Alice Jablonsky

Graphic Designers
Tanya Napier and Domini Dragoone

Illustrator
Shelly Meridith Delice

Editor
Erin Conley

Production Artist
Domini Dragoone

Created and produced by Orange Avenue Publishing
San Francisco, CA

A Girl's Guide to the
MARTIAL ARTS

TABLE OF CONTENTS

ANCIENT ORIGINS

The Warrior Princess Within You

Tired of the usual aerobics workout? Think the diva Pilates class your mom takes isn't quite your style? Then maybe it's time to get your kicks from something that really packs a punch!

We're talking about martial arts. Different types of martial arts are super hot these days, and you don't have to be Bruce Lee or one of Charlie's Angels to learn the basics. But learning a martial art is a bit more complicated than just putting on a sports bra and doing some jumping jacks.

Although martial artists do exercises, like stomach crunches and push-ups, the main part of training is learning the technique and discipline of the specific martial arts style. It's also about strength—your physical presence in the world. Even more important, though, it's about mind over matter, respect, and discipline—your feelings about yourself and the world around you. Plus, as with yoga, when you practice martial arts, you're stretching your mind and spirit as well as your body. The important martial arts values you need to remember are *respect, confidence, discipline, mental alertness, and a positive attitude.*

So, just what are martial arts? The martial arts we see and practice for fun and fitness today are based on ancient ways of fighting in countries like Japan, China, Korea, and the Philippines. These days, most martial arts are practiced as sports, exercise, or for self-defense. They're taught in special classes all over the world. Students start at the same level and, over many years, learn specific moves associated with a martial arts style.

Martial arts aren't something new, although some styles are newer than others. Martial arts can be traced back hundreds of years. In Japan, more than 700 years ago, Samurai warriors used jujitsu to protect the land and property of a shogun, the military leader of a region. Shaolin monks in China developed kung fu more than 1,500 years ago! As these arts were passed down to other people and other generations, new styles were created.

From Quiet Courage to Beautiful Warrior

Hey, if you think it was just guys that started martial arts, you're wrong. Long ago, a father had his daughter tutored as if she were a son. Jingyong (whose name meant Quiet Courage) studied art, literature, music, and medicine, but she excelled in martial arts. She learned to use her chi (or vital energy) as she studied kung fu. When neighboring warriors killed her family, Jingyong escaped and made her way to the Shaolin monastery where Buddhist monks had practiced kung fu for hundreds of years. To be welcomed at the monastery, Jingyong had to prove herself by accepting a challenge from one of the monks. To the surprise of everyone, Jingyong defeated him. She shaved her head, became a Shaolin nun, and was given the name Wu Mei, which means Beautiful Warrior. Wu Mei added and adapted kung fu moves and became a master, passing on her form of martial arts to other young women. Eventually, her style became known as Wing Chun kung fu after one of her female students.

ANCIENT ORIGINS

Which Style Is for You?

There are many different styles of martial arts. They're divided into hard and soft styles. Hard styles use power, speed, and high kicks. Soft styles use slow, flowing moves. In this book, you'll be introduced to six popular styles that fall on both sides of the exercise mat. These basic styles are likely to be taught in your neighborhood. After reading this book and getting an idea of what schools are available to you, you may want to take a class to develop your skills.

It's important to remember that styles vary from school to school and from instructor to instructor. Also, each style has many different substyles that may share the same basic techniques or philosophy but have different characteristics that make them unique. Therefore, you should visit several schools to observe a class. You'll also want to take time to talk with the instructor after class. Ask yourself these questions as you observe the class:

⇥ Is the instructor friendly?

⇥ Do the students show him respect?

⇥ Does s/he give individual attention when needed?

⇥ Does s/he show how and why students perform a specific move?

⇥ How many girls/women are in the class/school?

⇥ Does the instructor only talk and watch or does the instructor participate?

You may find instructors who prefer one style to another. However, don't let anyone tell you that one form of martial art is better for girls than another. The best one is the one that makes you feel comfortable. It's the one that generates self-confidence and inspires you to keep practicing.

When choosing a martial art for exercise, make sure the style you choose is the right one for your physical abilities. Some styles focus on one part of the body over another. In general, make sure your body—especially your lower back, knees, and ankles—can handle an hour of mega-exercise.

Read about the styles, and then observe and take a class. Whatever makes you feel good is a good place to begin. So let's get started!

Yin and Yang

The Chinese symbol for yin (soft) and yang (hard) represents the positive and negative life forces that hold the universe in balance. It shows yin and yang as opposites, like light and dark or heaven and earth. The symbol for yin is the dark side; the symbol for yang is the light side. The small circle of the opposite color inside the larger color tells us that yin and yang are both needed for harmony and balance. In martial arts, the symbol represents stillness and motion, hardness and softness. It means that both strength and control must be used.

Let's Get Physical

Hey! This is important! The fitness poses and techniques described in this book are presented to give you an introduction to several styles of martial arts. They are safe for the average person who is fit and who warms up properly before starting to exercise. Make sure you talk to your doctor before trying out any new fitness program. Don't push yourself trying to perform any of the exercises in this book. If you feel tired, dizzy, or pain, **STOP** and consult your doctor!

If you choose to learn a martial art, you'll benefit physically *and* mentally. For girls, practicing a martial art strengthens our legs and builds our upper bodies. Even less aggressive styles will give you a workout as energized as an aerobics class. As an added benefit to your physical conditioning, you'll probably experience a major attitude change. That's because martial arts also help you build character and grow as a person.

At first, trying to master even the very basics may seem complicated. Watch out for your thumb, place your arm at your hip, stretch your rear leg, stand straight, look forward, and keep your head up. Yikes! There's a lot to remember. But the more you practice, the more these positions and movements become second nature to you. Your body will automatically know what to do. Since different styles tend to favor some parts of the body over others, make sure you consider your strengths and weaknesses as you compare your favorite styles. Before undertaking any form of martial art, remember these important points:

→ Get a checkup! Ask your doctor if your knees, ankles, and lower back can handle an hour or more of challenging exercise.

→ Don't continue to exercise a weak joint. If you're in pain, you're putting too much stress on that part of your body.

→ Read about all the different martial arts styles, and find one that suits you.

→ Visit several schools before you settle on one.

→ Take classes from an experienced instructor.

→ And safety always comes first!

Ninja Angels

If you were a girl born into a ninja family 600 years ago in Japan, chances are you'd be taught, starting at age five or six, to be a super athlete, along with your brothers (if you had any). Ninja were like Japanese secret agents. They were awesome fighters who could disguise themselves so not even their own mothers would recognize them! Ninja used many different martial arts, including ninjutsu, which means "the art of stealth." They were like Spiderman, climbing and jumping from buildings and walls. They were so good at hiding that people thought they were able to make themselves invisible. Female ninja were called kunoichi and were trained in the same fighting techniques as the guys! Today, in Japan, the word "ninja" is used for a person who does undercover military operations.

What Comes First?

EXERCISE   Doing any kind of martial arts is going to mean sweat and effort to get in shape. So drop that remote and get going! Almost every martial arts class begins with exercises to warm up your muscles and get your heart rate up. You'll perform some simple body stretches as well as some old favorites—jumping jacks and stomach crunches! It's super important to warm up your muscles before you practice kicks and punches.

FOCUS   The center of your body is the place where your power lies. Your internal energy, or chi, originates from a place about two inches (five cm) below your belly button. From there, the energy flows through your legs, arms, and the rest of your body like a powerful chain. If you focus and feel centered, you'll increase your energy and power. Whether you punch or kick, all force is generated from your abs. A strong middle connects your upper and lower body. So, if your abs are weak, your power chain is broken.

BREATH If you take martial arts classes, you will be taught that breath control equals mind control. Breathing is one of the most important ways to gain energy. By remembering to breathe properly—inhaling through your nose and exhaling through your mouth—you're able to concentrate more and keep your energy level high. Right now, take a deep breath. Does your upper chest expand? If so, your normal day-to-day breathing is shallow and weak. When you breathe correctly, your stomach expands when you inhale. Breathing with your abdomen allows you to bring in more air. When you have more air, your energy level rises.

BALANCE You can tell a lot about a person by their body language. Most people watch TV slouched over a couch or in a chair. To generate energy while doing all of your daily activities—sitting, standing, or walking—you need to be centered and balanced. This means having both feet firmly rooted on the ground. When doing exercises, make sure you don't tip too far forward or backward or from side to side. Try to keep your weight on your rear foot until the forward foot has found a secure footing. This prevents you from losing your footing if the front foot finds unsteady or slippery ground.

Oops! There's a Dress Code

Yup, it's true. Your bare midriff and toe ring are fashion don'ts in martial arts class. Every martial art has its own uniform. Usually in beginning classes, all students—guys or girls—wear the same clothes to show they're equals. In Chinese kung fu, students may wear a *sam,* pants and a jacket, which are often black. In most cases, students wear a loose-fitting white cotton outfit when practicing. It may not look chic, but it's practical. The loose white pants and white cotton jacket are called a *gi* (pronounced GHEE in Japanese). Girls can also wear a white T-shirt underneath. For learning the basics in this book, comfy sweats and a T-shirt will be fine!

When you do finally decide to buy a traditional martial arts uniform, part of your outfit may be a colored belt around your waist to hold the jacket in place. Most martial arts have their own different colored belts for each level. Students earn colored belts as they learn new skills. The colors also help the instructor group students of equal skill safely for drills. In general, the order of the colors goes from lighter to darker as your skill level increases. In some schools, white belts are for new students. Yellow and green belts signify an intermediate skill level. A brown belt means you're at an advanced skill level. And a black belt means you've got game, girl!

One of the good things about a martial arts class is that you don't need much in the way of equipment or gadgets. All you need for basic training are your hands and feet. Most schools will have you practice barefoot so you can feel the floor. Required safety equipment depends on which style you're into. So, when you visit a school, make sure you ask the instructor what you'll need.

In Search of Chi: The Mind-Body Connection

Okay, so you've got the outfit down. That's just the outside, though. What's more important is what's inside, your inner strength. In Japan, it's called *ki* (pronounced KEE). In China, it's called *chi* (CHEE), which literally means "breath." In this book, we'll use the Chinese term most of the time.

So what exactly is chi? Chi is an energy—a force circulating through your body—that is nurtured by your mind. In fact, experts feel that girls make great martial artists because what we lack in strength, we more than make up for in mental ability.

If you're wondering if you have chi, the answer is yes. Everyone does. We sense people's energy every day. For example, if you're waiting in line for tickets to a show and someone stands too close, you might feel uncomfortable because your "space" has been invaded or maybe you're in math class and you get the feeling someone is staring at you. You look up from your desk to see that the boy in the next row is looking right at you! It's weird how we can sense things going on around us. Chi is recognizing that everything and everyone has that energy force.

The trick is to know how to tap into your chi, or inner strength, and *control it*. The ability to use your mind to control your body requires mental concentration and determination. This mental ability is the key to increasing your chi and succeeding in martial arts. You have to believe you can do something in order to achieve it. Then you have to combine belief with effort. So when you think of chi, remember that it isn't some magical power—it's thinking positive, believing in yourself, and having faith.

KUNG FU

So you want to be a **kung fu** diva? You can thank the movies for bringing martial arts into the spotlight. Kung fu teacher and actor Bruce Lee kicked it off with his kung fu fighting. But kung fu actually isn't the name of an individual martial art. Outside of China, kung fu refers to many styles. In China, it's known as *wushu*, and it's been around for thousands of years. Kung fu is a Chinese term that sort of means "effort" or "work," and you'll work your entire body practicing any of the styles. Many kung fu styles are tied to nature and are based on the movements of real and mythical animals, such as the monkey and the dragon.

Kung Fu 101

EXERCISES   Basic exercises are an important part of kung fu training. Techniques such as blocks, holds, throws, sweeps, and kicks are taught to develop the ability to defend yourself. Hand movements are choreographed patterns designed to build strength, speed, stamina, rhythm, and accuracy. Remember the mind-body connection when you do any warm-up exercises as well as when you practice your techniques. The mind affects the body, and the body affects the mind.

SPARRING   Sparring gives you the opportunity to test what you've learned with a partner. It also improves your reflexes and builds self-confidence. Light contact with your opponent may be made in some classes that are closely supervised. But we don't want you actually to punch or kick your girlfriend when practicing the basic moves featured in this book! Go through the movements slowly and gently. The illustrations and steps presented here are just to give you a feel for some of the techniques. When looking at martial arts clubs or classes, make sure they offer a noncontact method of sparring that doesn't require you to purchase extra equipment like a protective helmet.

STANCES A stance is simply the way you stand and hold your body, but it's one of the most important things you'll learn in kung fu or any other martial art. Mastering a stance will make it easier for you to concentrate on the other elements of the move. When practicing stances, you must start with good balance, so stand with your feet planted firmly in position.

The horse stance looks like—what else?—a person riding a horse. This posture will really condition your legs and buttocks. Keep your knees bent so your center of gravity is low. Move your feet about shoulder-width apart. Keep your knees bent slightly; you'll feel the tension in your outer thighs. Keep your shoulders relaxed, your back straight, and your bottom tucked in. But don't let your knees go over your toes. This stance looks easier than it is!

More About Stances

Kung fu stances, especially the horse stance, build strong leg power needed for kicking and moving quickly. A horse stance can be done in different ways, depending on what kick or block you have in mind. You can keep your knees just slightly bent for a quick response or go deep and low to maintain your balance. Either way, this stance will strengthen the lower muscles and joints of your body, especially your hips, knees, and ankles. The secret of practicing a stance is not to concentrate on the posture itself but on quickly moving from one stance to another. This positions you to deliver a strike or move out of the line of fire if your opponent is about to strike or kick you!

Blocks Kung fu stresses muscle strength, speed, and animated jumps. The various styles focus on energetic kicks and punches as well as some blocking techniques that don't seem to have much movement at all. A block is an arm or leg movement designed to stop or redirect your partner's incoming strike. Blocks are necessary in any martial art. Different types of blocks protect your head, body, or legs. You have to watch your partner closely to notice the angle and target area of incoming strikes.

X Block

This may seem like a pretty elementary move, but it's a critical one! The X block, or fork extended block, can protect either your head and face or your stomach and pelvis area. It lets both of your hands simultaneously protect against the incoming strike.

Upper X Block

1 Stand with your feet shoulder-width apart and your knees bent slightly.

2 Keep your arms bent and close to your sides with your fists facing palm up and resting on your hips.

3 To protect your head and face, form an X with both arms extended just above your head. The soft (or inner) part of your forearms should be facing away from you.

4 Keep your hands about four inches (10 cm) apart. It doesn't matter which hand is crossed over the other. Your elbows should be about 14 inches (35 cm) apart.

5 The contact area where the incoming strike will hit is where your arms and hands form the X.

Lower X Block

1 To protect the lower part of your body, form the X by extending both of your arms below your waist.

2 Turn your forearms in so the soft (or inner) part faces toward you.

3 Your hands should be about four inches (10 cm) apart and your elbows about 14 inches (35 cm) apart.

4 The contact area is where your arms and hands form the X.

Strikes & Punches
In kung fu, hand techniques differ greatly. Some blows are made with fists, and some are done with an open hand. Still others use your elbow or fingers. There are also many ways to make a fist that can help you respond easily and with little force.

Dragon's Head Punch

This punch is sometimes known as the middle knuckle punch or dragon's tooth punch. It's a thrust punch where the middle knuckle (the dragon's tooth) sticks out slightly from the rest of your fist. In kung fu sparring, the dragon's tooth punch can deliver a sharp blow that targets spots like the ribs, armpit, or neck.

1 Form a fist by folding all of your fingers into your palm. Your thumb should be on the outside of your knuckles.

2 Raise the first joint of your middle finger so it sticks out from your fist.

3 Hold your thumb tightly below your middle finger as support.

4 Stand facing your partner with your feet parallel and shoulder-width apart. Take a step forward and slightly out with your left leg into a front stance.

5 Bend your arms and rest your fists (palm side up) on your hips. Make sure your middle knuckle is raised in the dragon's tooth position.

6 As you reach up toward your partner's neck, rotate your arm slightly so your fist and knuckle lightly touch your partner's neck. Keep your elbow bent.

7 Rotate your arm back and return it to the original position, resting on your hip.

Developing Your Punch

One thing to remember is to always keep your punching arm slightly bent. You should learn to punch with both your right and left hands. However, for the purposes of this book, most of the techniques focus on right-hand movements.

Wing Chun Punch

The Wing Chun style of kung fu was developed by a woman over 300 years ago. Pretty impressive, huh? Its moves are fast, powerful, and efficient. Most experts consider this particular basic kung fu punch to be the most effective hand-to-hand combat punch because it's the most direct. The important thing to remember is that your wrist is never bent. It's held straight so the bones on the back of your hand are aligned with your wrist and forearm.

1 Position your legs in a forward stance. Start with your feet parallel and shoulder-width apart.

2 Step forward and out slightly with your left leg. Keep both knees bent.

3 Guard the centerline of your body by holding your fists up like a boxer and your elbows down and close to your body.

4 As you aim at your imaginary target, extend your right arm in a direct, straight line. Don't extend your arm completely or lock your elbow.

5 Your fist should be vertical at the point of contact so that the bottom three knuckles touch your opponent.

6 Alternate your right and left arms as you move toward your target, making quick and short punches.

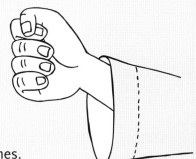

Kicks

Kung fu kicks are usually low and swift. When preventing a strike from an opponent's kick, be sure to turn your kicking foot out to the side to gain greater surface area for contact. Because kicking involves so many muscles, make sure to warm up and stretch before attempting any kick!

Roundhouse Kick

This circular kick uses the ball of your foot to make contact. The power of this kick is generated by completely turning your hips. The idea is to push your opponent off balance and throw her body backward, creating more distance between the two of you. When executing a roundhouse kick, don't allow the knee of your kicking leg to swing beyond your supporting leg. Otherwise, you could lose your own balance and land on your bottom!

1 Stand in a ready stance—with your feet shoulder-width apart and your knees bent slightly.

2 Hold your forearms out in front of your chest, with your fists facing each other. Your right arm should be slightly higher than your left.

3 Shift your weight to your left leg and lift your right leg, sort of like a flamingo. Your ankle should be positioned next to your left knee.

4 Keeping your leg bent, move your whole leg back so that it is parallel to the floor with your foot facing backward.

5 Pivot on the ball of your left foot so that it turns out to the left. At the same time, extend your right leg toward your imaginary target.

6 Pull your right leg back into its coiled position.

7 Return your right foot to the ground.

KARATE

Karate originated 600 years ago on the island of Okinawa, Japan. After a struggle with a neighboring land, those in power took away all of the weapons on the island. To protect themselves, Okinawans created a secret style of fighting using their arms and legs. Because no weapons were used, the style of fighting was called karate, or "empty hand." This way of fighting soon made its way to the rest of Japan, where it developed into a form of physical training and a popular sport. Like all martial arts, karate contains a variety of styles each with its own differences. No matter which style you learn, you'll get an incredible all-around workout!

Things You Should Know

HOW TO STAND Most martial arts teach a similar ready stance, or way to stand. Usually, your feet are spread wide, your knees are bent, and your body weight is evenly distributed. In karate, when you block an attack or deliver a punch, often one or both of your arms are pulled back as if floating on your hip bones. This is called the chamber position. One arm moves out either to meet the target or to cut off the attack while the other arm is pulled back to the chamber position. Arm movements are done simultaneously and with super speed, of course!

Karate students must also learn to balance on one leg to deliver kicks. The cat stance places more weight on the back leg so the front leg can strike out with a kick. Other stances place the weight on the front leg so you can kick out with the back leg.

HOW TO MAKE A FIST To make a proper fist, bend the middle and top knuckles inward so that your fingertips reach the base of your fingers (where they join the palm). Continue to fold your fingers inward so they press against your palm. Keeping your wrist straight (so that it is even with the top of the fist), fold

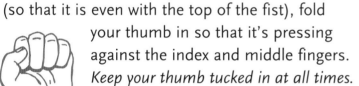

your thumb in so that it's pressing against the index and middle fingers. *Keep your thumb tucked in at all times.*

A basic fist is used in attacking and defending exercises. In attack position, keep your wrist pointing forward and in a straight line with your arm. Don't flex your fist up or down at your wrist. Strike with the front of the first two knuckles. For blocking, this position helps prevent injury to your thumb and fingers.

Make sure all punches and kicks begin at the hips. In other words, put your whole body into it! This will give you extra power and protect your muscles.

The Karate Way

The point in karate is to deliver powerful kicks, punches, and blocks using your arms and legs. It can be forceful and loud. Although you won't actually be striking your partner, you might feel compelled to scream. Many people scream "KIAI!" (or some other distracting yell from deep inside their belly) when they practice delivering a powerful blow. However, karate also uses defensive moves like blocks and kicks. Karate teaches you how to move your body by hopping, sliding, or turning. In other words, you learn to become a moving target!

Blocks Blocking is when one part of your body is used to stop or redirect a move aimed at another part of your body. Blocks protect against punches to your head, stomach, or lower body. Although protecting yourself against an opponent is your first priority, a good block can also provide an opportunity for a counterstrike.

Upward Block

The upward block is the basic block used to prevent a blow directed to the upper part of your body. Think of a strike coming at you about nose level, just under your eyes. Your nose and eyes are the most sensitive places on your head. So, if you were to get hit in either place, it would painful. This sort of distraction is just the opportunity a karate fighter is looking for.

1 Stand in a ready stance with your knees bent and feet shoulder-width apart.

2 Bend your elbows and cross your forearms in front of your chest. It doesn't matter which arm is on top.

3 Place both fists up so that your thumbs are facing toward you.

4 Pull your right elbow back and down with your wrist facing palm side up. Your right forearm will be near your waist and parallel to the floor.

5 At the same time, begin rotating your left elbow and lifting your forearm. Your left fist will be in front of your forehead, or slightly higher, with the back of your hand facing your body.

6 To complete the block, rotate both forearms back into their set position.

Blocking Techniques

Many different types of blocks are used in karate. Two general groups are sweeping blocks and impact blocks. The upward block (on the previous page) is an example of a sweeping block. It doesn't require a lot of force to stop or redirect the punch. The elbow block is an impact block. In a real sparring situation, the force of your elbow would meet the force of your partner's hand. Ouch!

Elbow Block

This type of block is basically a collision between your elbow and your partner's hand or fist. When your partner tries to deliver a strike or punch, your elbow is there to block and throw her off balance. Make sure you twist your body so that your side is facing your partner. This twisting movement gives added speed and force to your block.

1 Start in a horse stance with knees bent and feet shoulder-width apart.

2 Bend your elbows, and bring your forearms close to your sides, resting on your hips.

3 Twist your torso sharply to the left. Your feet should remain in the set position.

4 As you twist your body, lift up your right elbow, turning your fist in a downward motion.

5 Block with the side of your right elbow.

you

Punches Just because you're a girl doesn't mean you can't deliver a powerful punch. In this exercise, as with others, you will not actually be striking your opponent but going through the stances that would lead up to a punch. Start by making a proper fist with your thumb *outside* your fingers. Basic punches begin from the standard chamber position. Your fists are closed and resting against your rib cage. Your palms face up and your elbows should be back against your ribs.

Straight Punch

The straight punch, sometimes known as the corkscrew punch, is delivered in a straight line right at your target. The force begins at your hip, powers through your arm, and then snaps out and back with lightning speed. It's important to remember that when you deliver this punch, your arm should only extend about 95 percent. This allows you to snap your arm back quickly and also prevents injury to your joints.

1 Start in the horse stance with knees bent and feet shoulder-width apart.

2 Both fists should be in chamber position, with fists closed and resting against your rib cage and your palms face up.

3 Rotate your right arm halfway around to the left. At the end of the punch, your forearm should be outstretched and facing down. Your fist should begin twisting as your elbow moves past your hip.

4 Move your fist in a straight line toward your target. Keep your elbows close to your body. If your elbows stick out, you'll lose power and speed.

5 As you deliver the punch, your shoulders and hips should stay parallel. Keep your attacking right fist in line with your right hip as you aim at your target.

6 Rotate your arm back to the right as you bring your fist back to its starting position.

Kicks

A kick is a good self-defense movement. It needs to be fast to catch your partner off guard so she doesn't have time to block the kick. Just like punches, the hips are the center for delivering kicks with force and power. There are two basic kinds of kicks. Snap kicks shoot out and immediately snap back. This allows you to deliver a series of quick kicks. With a thrust kick, you aim for your target, then hold for a second to deliver the power.

Front Snap Kick

This basic karate kick begins in a forward stance, which makes it hard for your partner to knock you off balance. It's important to keep your weight centered on the balls of your feet for balance as you move quickly around the training mat. When you're ready to kick, keep your foot in a straight line with your leg and strike with the ball of the foot.

1 Place your feet shoulder-width apart in a forward stance. Your left leg should be forward, and your right leg should be back and slightly positioned away from your hip. Make sure your feet are pointed forward. Keep your left (forward) knee bent and directly over your left heel.

2 To help maintain your balance, bend your arms so your hands are on your hips.

3 Begin your kick by shifting your weight to your left leg and bringing your bent knee up as high as you can in front of you.

4 Turn your toes up so your point of contact will be the ball of your foot.

5 Extend your right leg into a nearly straight line, but keep your knee bent slightly. If you were really facing an opponent, this could prevent you from getting injured if she were to try to block your kick. Keep your toes turned up (not pointed forward), and breathe out.

6 Snap your foot back into position so it's once again pointed toward the ground with your right knee bent and most of your weight centered on your left leg.

7 Set your foot back into the original forward stance position.

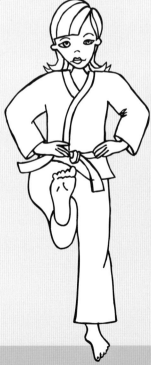

The Korean martial art of **tae kwon do** means "way of the foot and hand." Its roots go back about 1,600 years, but the art we practice today was developed in the 1950s. There are different styles of tae kwon do—even an Olympic style that emphasizes sparring—but they all feature high kicks, punching, and blocks. Once the techniques are learned, students put them together to create a *form*, which is a set pattern of moves students memorize and practice. Training in tae kwon do has tons of mental and physical benefits. Just taking a beginner class will help you become more fit and, of course, help get rid of stress.

Step Sparring

In this book, we're focusing on the physical and mental fitness of martial arts training, and this includes building your self-confidence. To help this process along, many martial arts teachers will have you work with a partner so you get used to having someone opposite you as you learn countermoves. This is called sparring. Training this way boosts your self-confidence in case you ever find yourself in a real self-defense situation. It also sharpens your reflex actions. Tae kwon do training can involve a lot of what is called step sparring, which prepares you for freestyle sparring. The main purpose of step sparring is to teach mobility and distance. In other words, you need to be nimble and fast to get close enough to deliver a strike and to move away quickly enough to avoid one. Although tae kwon do step sparring is done in class under close teacher supervision, don't be surprised if you still manage to end up with a few bruises! Remember, when practicing the moves in this book, don't actually punch or kick your partner!

Stance Secrets

Stances are important to get your body into the proper position before practicing a technique. They're also great stretching exercises. Stances focus first on your feet and legs and second on your hands and arms.

The fighting stance, also called a back stance or L stance, is when knees are only slightly bent, which allows you to move around more quickly. Point your right foot forward. Turn your hips and chest toward the side. Your weight should be almost evenly distributed between your legs but with slightly more weight on your back leg. Bend your left arm at chest level, and hold your right arm in striking position.

You'll find that most blocks are made using a fist. However, sometimes you can use an open hand where your palm and fingers are straight. This is called a knife hand because the edge of the hand shapes itself into a knife. Whether you use a fist or a knife hand, your thumb needs to be tucked in to give support and prevent injury.

Mega Power Moves

In tae kwon do, you'll learn to stretch and exercise nearly every muscle group in your body. That aspect alone distinguishes the sport from most others. Emphasis on improved concentration, stamina, and self-control is what really sets tae kwon do apart from other martial arts. If there's a formula for power in tae kwon do, it's **TECHNIQUE + SPEED = POWER**. With repetition and practice you'll learn the technique. Then you'll work to add speed to your moves, which generates power.

Blocks In tae kwon do, there are lots of different types of blocks used to thwart a punch or a kick. After tons of practice hours, the movements almost become automatic. All blocks are taught and then practiced with the aid of step sparring. Step sparring allows you to work on accuracy and become more comfortable with someone nearly punching you in the face!

Low Block

The low block is the first block a beginner learns. For this block to work, it must come from high to low and the fist must twist at the end.

1 Start in a ready stance, feet shoulder-width apart. Then move your right leg a shoulder-width forward in front of your left leg.

2 Cross your arms in front of your chest with the right arm on the inside, palm facing toward you. Your left palm should face away from you.

3 Swing your right arm down in a diagonal sweeping motion across your body. Your right hand should be palm down, over your right leg, and just over the middle of your right thigh. Your fist should not touch your leg.

4 As you execute the block, pull your left fist back to your waist, twisting to palm side up. This is called the reaction hand. The harder you pull this hand back to your waist, the stronger your other hand will block and punch. In tae kwon do, this position is called the home of the fist.

5 Your left hand is now ready to punch, if necessary.

Inside-Out Crescent Block

The crescent block is an example of a sweeping block. Although you don't need a lot of force to stop a strike coming your way, you need to remember *not* to swing your arm out to your side. Keep your elbow pointed straight and forward. A good way to check your position is to bring your fist toward your shoulder. If your arm is positioned incorrectly, your fist will move toward your head.

1 Begin in a back or L stance with legs shoulder-width apart and knees bent. Face your right leg and body forward, and your left leg back and toward the left.

2 Your arms should be in chamber position with elbows bent, crossing in front of your chest. Your left forearm should be on top of your right. Turn your palms so your fists are facing down.

3 Swing your right forearm up and to the right, across the front of your body at chest level with the fist palm up. Pretend you're sweeping a fan-shaped area in front of your face.

4 At the same time, pull back your left arm so it's at your waist, knuckles facing the floor.

5 Your right (blocking) arm should be bent at a 90 degree angle at your elbow. The palm of your fist should be facing toward you.

Strikes The art of striking includes many different ways to use your hands. In tae kwon do, you use different areas of your hand to deliver a strike. Each type of strike is meant for a different target on your opponent. Learning the proper way to hold your hand—as well as your arm and body—with each different strike gives you the maximum power behind each hand motion you deliver.

Fingertip Thrust

This strike, sometimes called a hand spear, looks like the basic karate chop you see in all those action movies. The hand spear is an open-handed move that's used in many styles of martial arts. Although the most effective use of your hand is delivering a punch with your fist, the hand spear is a good self-defense technique when you want to aim for the eyes, below the nose, the ribs, and the chest.

1 Begin in a ready stance with your feet shoulder-width apart and your knees bent.

2 Extend the fingers on your right hand, and keep them close together. (Some instructors may have you bend your middle finger slightly so that it's even with your other two fingers.)

3 Fold your thumb into the base of your fingers.

4 To strike with your right hand, step forward with your right leg.

5 While keeping your arm straight, pretend to strike your target gently using the tips of your three longest fingers.

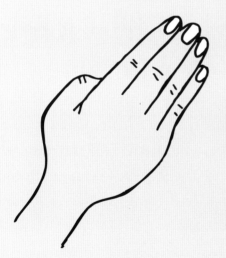

Kicks Tae kwon do is a good martial art for girls because of the emphasis on kicking. (Kicks are generally more powerful than punches.) Girls are often more flexible than boys, so we're able to manage the gymnastics moves more easily. As you train, you'll learn to use different parts of your feet for different types of kicks. You'll also learn how to put your full body weight behind each kick. Each type of kick is intended for a different target on your opponent.

Side Kick

There are three basic kicks found in many martial arts: front snap, side kick, and roundhouse. The side kick is one of the first kicks you'll learn. Once you're able to master all three, your teacher will move you up to the flying variations. The side kick is taught from a fighting stance. The kick itself comes straight out from the body and off the front leg.

1 Position yourself in a horse stance, with feet parallel and shoulder-width apart, and knees bent.

2 Both arms should be chambered close to your sides, elbows bent, and fists palm up.

3 Bring your right knee up as high as possible. Flex your right foot so the heel points toward the ground. Pivot your back foot so your toes point away from your opponent and your heel points toward her. This opens up your hips and will help you deliver a higher kick.

4 Raise the hip of your supporting leg and turn the foot outward away from the direction of the kick.

5 Extend your right leg straight at your target or opponent, thrusting your hip into the attack at the same time. (The power should be concentrated on the edge of your foot.) Exhale as you deliver the strike. Remember not to take your eyes off of your target!

6 Pull your right knee and leg back, and set your right foot back into the starting position.

Jujitsu is one of Japan's oldest forms of martial arts. There are many different styles, but most have common techniques of defending yourself with kicks, punches, blocks, throws, takedowns, and jointlocks and by targeting pressure points. Your ability to move from one technique to another as needed is at the heart of jujitsu. In schools, jujitsu is presented as a self-defense martial art. One school might emphasize throwing techniques while another might focus on kicks and punches. No matter which techniques you learn in jujitsu, you'll get a super workout as you increase your flexibility and tone up your muscles!

The Way of the Samurai

Hundreds of years ago, Japanese warriors known as samurai were recruited from the young men of prominent families. They were taught the arts as well as archery and swordsmanship. To be a samurai, you had to be born into a family that had samurai history. The soldiers were armed with a sword and often went to a special school for training.

Along with armed combat, samurai practiced a style of jujitsu. It was incorporated into the samurai warrior's training and was used together with his weapon. Because of the code of discipline, loyalty, and respect they learned, samurai warriors were proud of their martial arts training.

Jujitsu Strategies

As a beginner, you will be learning jujitsu without weapons. When training in jujitsu, remember that some of it's physical and some of it's psychological, but these two aspects go hand in hand.

- →→ Speed is better than power. You want to take your partner by surprise.

- →→ Don't overextend your strike. Extending a strike too far will throw you off balance and make you vulnerable to attacks.

- →→ Manage the distance between yourself and your partner so that you can attack her but she can't attack you effectively.

- →→ Make small movements; the larger your movements, the larger the opening you provide for your partner to attack you.

- →→ Regulate your own timing, rhythm, and speed. Don't get locked into your partner's timing.

- →→ Stay mobile and fluid. Remember to relax and stay focused.

- →→ Always exhale when striking. This gives you more power.

- →→ Hang in there. No matter how many times you fall, keep getting up and pursuing your goal!

The "Gentle Art"—May the Force Be With You!

Although jujitsu is known as the "gentle art," it might not seem so tame when used for self-defense. The basic principle behind most jujitsu movements is to redirect a strike, a kick, or a throw delivered by your opponent. In other words, it's better to use the force directed against you rather than trying to block it with your own force. Sound like you're training to be a Jedi knight? It's not so far off. The key is to throw your opponent off balance by using her own force against her. By using jujitsu techniques, you can learn to disable a bigger, heavier, and stronger opponent with a throw, a well-placed kick, or a strike.

Break Falls
When you practice jujitsu, you need to learn how to fall without getting hurt. This means you'll practice break falls. It's best to start low and slow. As your training progresses, you can increase the height and speed of your fall. You should practice with something soft, like a bunch of pillows or a mattress. Besides being necessary when training in jujitsu, knowing break falls will come in handy if you happen to fall somewhere else!

Sideways Break Fall

Because learning to fall is a way to protect yourself, you'll need to learn break falls that go forward, backward, and sideways. All of them can be adapted to help you fall in any direction as long as you follow the basic principles.

1 Begin by squatting at the edge of a padded floor. As a beginner, start from a low position, and gradually work up to a standing position.

2 Tuck your head into your right shoulder.

3 Cross your right leg in front of your left leg to throw yourself off balance, and fall to the right side.

4 Just as your right shoulder and side hit the floor, slap the floor with your left forearm. This way, the impact of the fall is spread over as wide an area as possible.

Important Stuff to Remember

- Tuck your chin into your chest, and turn your head to the side to prevent your head from hitting the mat.

- Keep your back curved.

- Never cross your feet as you fall. Crossing your feet can cause injury to your shoulder.

- Strike the mat hard with your forearms and palms.

Blocking Techniques

How you're taught blocks may vary slightly. However, they're all taught for the same reasons:

⇒ To change the direction of your partner's attack.

⇒ To make contact with your target near your elbow instead of your wrist.

⇒ To use speed more than power.

⇒ To read your partner's objectives before she delivers a blow.

⇒ To throw your partner off balance, allowing you to counterattack.

Left High Parry

A block is designed to stop the momentum of an intended strike. A parry is a type of block that redirects the force of the attack away from you. This a good defensive move because it's easy to learn. The left high parry ends with your open hand next to your partner's wrist and close enough to your body so you can launch into a quick counterattack. If you don't have a partner, practice your moves in front of a mirror.

1 Stand facing your partner. Both of you should be facing forward with your feet parallel.

2 Have your partner step forward with her right foot and pretend to deliver a punch to your face (at about nose level) with her right fist.

3 To do the parry, step forward and out slightly to the left with your left foot.

4 As you step, extend your left hand forward. Your hand should be opened and in front of your left shoulder.

5 Quickly sweep the back of your left hand across your body to your right shoulder.

6 As you do that, your left palm should make contact with the outside of your partner's right wrist.

7 Your left palm should redirect the punch just past your face.

you

Strikes A strike refers to an open-handed blow, a thrust refers to an open-handed blow with a push, and a punch usually means your hand is in a fist. No matter what you call it, understanding how to strike "through" your target is important. If your target is your partner's chin, aim for the back of her head. This way, were you actually to hit her chin, your strike would continue to move "through" the target. This is how martial arts masters generate the power needed to hit a target effectively.

Palm Heel Strike

One very simple but powerful blow with the hand is the palm heel strike. (The palm heel is the very bottom part of your palm.) In many ways, this can be a more effective blow than a punch because it doesn't take a lot of training to learn. You are also less likely to injure your hand than with a punch. This strike is especially effective when your partner is in front of you or when you want to move her away from you. If you ever need to use this move in a real self-defense situation, good target areas are the jaw, nose, ear, or under the chin.

1 Face your partner, and stand about three feet (1 m) apart.

2 Begin in a forward stance with your feet shoulder-width apart. Move your right leg forward.

3 Place your right hand in the chamber position—palm up, fingers extended and held tightly together.

4 Hold your left palm out straight, and keep your fingers straight and together, centered on your partner's body, at nose height.

5 Extend your right hand forward. Your right hand should be flexed so that your fingers are out of the way. (Just pretend you're a waiter carrying a tray of food!)

6 Stop when your arm is almost fully extended. It should be centered on your partner's body at nose height. At the same time, retract your left arm into the chamber position, rotating your hand so that your palm is facing up.

7 Keep the base of your right palm heel turned up.

8 Follow through by driving your palm heel toward the center of your partner's face—just remember to stop short of actually hitting her!

you

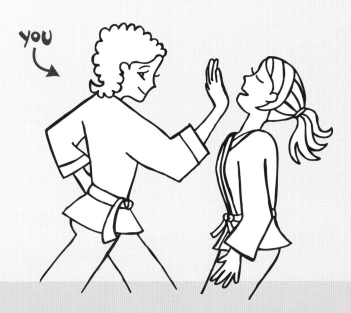

Throws Once you learn how to do break falls, you'll be ready to throw your partner. When practicing jujitsu with a partner, the teacher will designate one person as the thrower and the other person the "throwee." An important part of throwing is to remember to keep your center of gravity lower than your partner's. To do this, keep your belt lower than your partner's belt as you throw. Each school will focus on different throws.

Outer Reaping Throw

This throw is found in many styles of jujitsu. Although the throw is broken down into individual steps, it's performed as one movement. The key to this is to break your partner's balance. Then, move into her so she can't regain her balance. Finally, carry out the throw. To perform this throw, you'll use your hands, feet, legs, and hips.

1 Begin with the traditional jujitsu grab. You will be the thrower, and your partner will be the throwee. Both partners should stand facing each other with feet shoulder-width apart. Each person's left foot is slightly ahead of the right.

2 Each partner should grab the other's left lapel with the right hand. Then both of you should grab each other's right elbow with your left hand.

3 To execute the throw, gently push your partner's head with your right hand while still holding onto her lapel. Your right hand will be on the left side of her face near her ear.

4 At the same time, pull down on your partner's right sleeve. This movement will throw her off balance so she'll step backward and onto her right leg.

5 As soon as you've knocked her off balance, hook your right foot behind her right knee with your heel. Keep your right foot and toes pointed down.

6 Follow through by kicking your right leg (the leg doing the hook) behind your partner's right knee and throwing her into a left sideways break fall.

you

AiKiDO

Although somewhat based on jujitsu, **aikido** is a modern Japanese martial art that was developed in the early 1900s. It's unlike some of the other martial arts you've been introduced to in this book because it focuses on defense instead of offense. The *O Sensei* (great teacher) who developed aikido wanted a way for people to settle conflicts peacefully. With aikido, you learn to defend yourself without hurting your opponent. However, it does teach you to use your hands to neutralize your partner's force. As a student of aikido, you'll increase your energy and self-control. It's also a great way to stay in shape!

Learning to Fall

In aikido, as in jujitsu, one of the first things you'll need to learn is how to break fall. You'll probably be hitting the mat a lot and falling in every possible direction, so you might as well be really good at it! If you're thrown onto the mat, one way to cushion your fall is to slap the mat with your hand. It's sort of like a shock absorber. For practice, crouch on the floor with your arms bent and crossed in front of you. Then, fall backward, chin tucked in, and arms unfolding, ending with a slap of your hands on the mat. By the time you practice break falling in different directions, your hands will definitely feel the sting!

Learning Not to Fall

When you're ready to throw someone down onto the mat, you need to be prepared to prevent yourself from being thrown. Stand with your feet shoulder-width apart and your knees bent slightly. Your body should be straight with your weight evenly distributed. To keep from being thrown, lower your center of gravity by bending your knees more. This position plants your feet firmly on the ground, making it difficult to catch you off balance.

You Go, Girl!

There are some advantages to being a girl when you practice aikido. That's because guys may have size and muscle power over us, but we're usually more flexible. Girls are also more intuitive than guys—in other words, we tap into our feelings more. That's an advantage. We're more likely to anticipate our partner's moves and avert them before making an offensive strike.

The longer you practice aikido, the more you'll perfect these qualities. In the meantime, speed, mobility, and balance are the strengths you'll need to work toward in your aikido training.

The "Way of Harmony"

In aikido, it's important to train the mind and spirit as well as the body. Aikido is a martial art and therefore facing an opponent is part of it. However, instead of using power to block a move, you use your ki (the Japanese word for your internal energy) to dodge it. The foundation of aikido is circular movements that unify the body, mind, and ki. This unification leads to harmony and spiritual growth. The key thing to remember is never to use strength against strength. The goal is to turn your partner's energy back on her. You have to use her weapons—her speed, power, and size—to your benefit.

Throws When you begin your aikido training, you'll practice with a partner. One of you will be the aggressor and the other the defender. Then you'll switch roles. An important move you'll learn is how to throw a partner off balance to defeat her. Many moves in aikido are circular. This enables you to keep your balance while your partner loses hers.

Wrist Lock

When doing this move, keep your hands at waist level for better leverage and control. Begin doing the steps very slowly until you are comfortable with the pattern. As you master each movement, you can increase your speed. The technique described here will position you as the defender. **Remember, it's very important to move slowly and gently whenever you practice this move or others in which pressure is applied to a part of the body!**

1 Stand facing your partner. Her feet should be shoulder-width apart.

2 You should stand in a forward stance—feet shoulder-width apart with your right foot ahead of your left.

3 Your partner should extend her right arm as if to push you in the chest.

4 Grab your partner's right wrist with both of your hands. Turn her palm so that it faces up, and bend her arm toward her right shoulder.

5 Slowly and gently press your thumbs into her hand (while still holding her arm with both of your hands).

6 Apply just enough pressure to bring her to her knees, but don't hurt your partner while doing this exercise!

YOU

Break Falls

As a beginning aikido student, you'll practice your break falls over and over until you can do them in your sleep. You have to be able to go into a break fall without even thinking. That's because you usually don't have time to think when your partner performs a surprise move. Your mind and your body need to know how to respond together, automatically. In aikido, as in jujitsu, you need to develop flexibility, balance, coordination, speed, and stamina. You also need to learn how to fall in any and all directions.

Backward Break Fall

This basic skill is one of first falls you'll learn in aikido. When doing any type of break fall, it's important to remember to keep your mouth closed and teeth together. Otherwise you might end up biting your tongue or cheek. Be sure to practice break falls on a padded mattress or mat until your body is conditioned.

1 Begin by squatting at the edge of your padded floor (don't forget pillows or a mattress).

2 Tuck your head in by bringing your chin close to your chest.

3 Cross your arms in front of your chest.

4 Curve your back and roll backward. Your shoulders should be on the floor.

5 As your shoulders come in contact with the floor, slap the floor with your palms and forearms. This will prevent you from continuing to roll backward and will also help absorb the impact of the fall.

6 Once you've had lots of practice and feel comfortable, you can gradually increase the height of your fall.

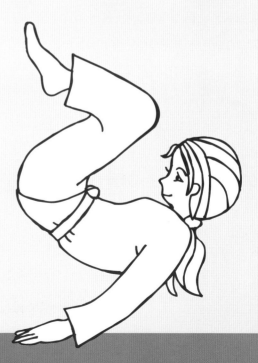

Rollouts

A good way to dodge your partner is to do a rollout. A rollout is an alternative to a break fall, but it accomplishes the same goal—protecting your body as you get out of the way and then regroup to launch a counterstrike. Remember, when someone is coming at you, your body will tend to go into crisis mode, which means you're likely to freak out. Instead, remember to breathe, relax, and drop into a lower stance to give yourself more balance ... or just roll out of the way!

Forward Rollout

The forward rollout is a way to move your body out of the way of your partner's aggressive action. You can practice this skill without a partner.

1 Start in a standing position.

2 To begin the rollout, step out with your right foot.

3 Your head should be tucked in so that your chin almost touches your chest.

4 As you begin to fall forward, form a circle with your arms over your head.

5 Roll forward on your shoulders and your upper back.

6 As you add momentum to this exercise, the extra speed will help you get to your feet without using your hands.

Blocks In most martial art styles, the first thing you want to do when you see an incoming punch or grab is to block it. You can do this by blocking the incoming blow with your free hand or fist or by redirecting the strike. This is the main principle behind the self-defense technique of aikido as well as jujitsu. It allows you time to aim your blow at a more sensitive part of your opponent's body. Blocking can be done with any part of your legs or arms but using your forearms is easiest.

Downward Inside Forearm Block

This block is effective when your opponent tries to deliver a strike or a kick to the lower part of your body or your legs. It sweeps away your partner's leg or arm with your forearm. Since your forearm is long, you don't have to worry too much about how accurate your block is. However, do try to have your forearm in a vertical position! This way, when you make contact with your partner's leg or arm, the hit will be closer to your wrist.

1 Face your partner and stand in a forward stance—legs shoulder-width apart with your left leg slightly ahead of your right.

2 Your fists should be in the chamber position so they're floating on your hips.

3 Have your partner move forward slowly and gently to level a kick at your lower body.

4 With your elbow slightly bent, sweep your left arm down across the lower part of your body.

5 Your forearm should make contact with your partner's leg, which will throw her off balance and leave her open for a counterattack.

6 When practicing this skill, make sure you and your partner start off slowly. Once you're familiar with the movement, you can increase your speed. Take turns so that both of you can practice blocking and kicking.

TAi CHi CHUAN

Most people think of **tai chi** as a slow-moving exercise routine that people do in the park to relax and meditate. In fact, this style is known as a soft martial art, where control over an opponent is gained by harnessing your internal energy, or chi. Unlike other martial arts styles, tai chi focuses on slowing down and paying attention to your body. It uses the principle of chi flowing through your body to increase strength, stamina, and flexibility. Don't let the smooth, fluid pace of tai chi fool you. Tai chi chuan, which means "supreme ultimate fist," is also an effective self-defense system.

Martial Art or Exercise Routine?

In tai chi classes, many students don't even realize that they're learning a martial art. The slow, graceful movements in tai chi seem to be so opposite from a punch or a kick. Remember yin and yang? Yin represents softness and yang represents hardness. As a martial art, tai chi uses both elements to achieve harmony and balance.

Whether for just plain exercise or for self-defense, each tai chi movement has a purpose, so it's important to understand how the movements all connect when you face an imaginary opponent. First, visualize your movement in your mind. How you move is exactly related to the direction of your body, the coordination of your legs and arms, your breathing, and the flow of chi through your body. The more you practice visualizing yourself against an invisible opponent, the better you will be at carrying out the moves.

With regular practice, tai chi can calm your mind and strengthen your body. All you need is energy, focus, and a peaceful environment.

Raising Your Chi Level

Doing some simple exercises can raise your level of chi. The more control over this internal energy you have, the more control you have over your body and your concentration. To begin, stand with your feet shoulder-width apart and your knees slightly bent. Your hands should be at your sides, fingers together, with your palms facing backward.

Bend your knees, and breathe in as you slowly raise your hands to chest level. Keep your arms relaxed and bent slightly. Now take a deep breath through your nose. Focus your mind on imagining chi entering your body. Breathe slowly out of your mouth and gently lower your hands.

As your hands reach their starting position, straighten your knees. Do ten repetitions of this exercise to raise your chi and gain control.

Go With the Flow

When first being introduced to tai chi chuan, most students will learn how to do solo exercises. These exercises, called postures, have really cool names, for example Embrace Tiger and Return to Mountain or Step Forward to the Seven Stars. As you become more advanced in your training, you'll learn how to work against real opponents using the solo postures. The key to tai chi self-defense is the ability to sense the flow of energy in your opponent; in other words, to anticipate the move she's about to make and prevent it before it's completed.

Movements & Forms

Tai chi movements are exercises done in slow motion to improve the flow of chi through your body. Each movement has a name and a meaning and can be strung together with other movements into a set pattern called a form. The number of movements in a form can be few or many. Tai chi is a beautiful martial art, and looks graceful and flowing.

Scooping the Sea

As you extend your hands and lean forward in this movement, think of all the fish you can gather from the sea. Focus on sending energy through your arms and out your fingers. As you draw back your arms, forget the fish and scoop up all the energy you can.

1 Stand with your feet shoulder-width apart and parallel. Your knees should be bent slightly, and your arms should be by your sides. Breathe out.

2 Take a step forward with your left foot and shift your weight onto it. Your right leg should be straight with your foot on the floor. Stretch your arms out in front of you.

3 Breathe in as you begin to shift your weight back from your left to your right foot. Open and draw back your arms.

4 Lean forward. At the same time, bring your hands together and ahead of your left knee. Bend your knee further, but don't allow it to go over the toes of your left foot.

5 Look up as you open your arms wide.

6 Return to the starting position, and repeat with the right leg.

Push Hands

This movement has been called a physical dialogue of pressure and withdrawal between you and your opponent. Each person uses only one hand. It helps you feel your opponent's balance and chi as she interacts with you. As you move with your partner's force, you prevent her chi from being used against you. The idea is to find a point where your opponent is off balance. Then, with just a little bit of pressure, you can tip her over.

1 Begin in a front stance with your right foot forward. Distribute your weight so that about 60 percent is on your right (front) foot and 40 percent is on your left (rear) foot.

2 Face your partner, and stand about three feet (1 m) apart. Extend your right arm at chest height. Your opponent should mirror your position.

3 Use your palm and make contact with the back of your partner's right wrist. At the same time, shift your weight onto your back (left) leg. Your partner should shift her weight onto her front (right) leg.

4 Maintain contact with your partner's wrist as you shift your weight forward onto your right foot. As your partner senses the pressure of your weight shift, she should move her body backward, turning her hand outward and twisting it to redirect your push. Keep swapping roles so that you each yield and push in turn, maintaining your balance.

5 As the entire sequence is repeated, you're creating one smooth, circular, and continuous figure eight movement with your hands.

6 Don't apply pressure with your hands; keep your body relaxed. Try to read your partner's energy.

7 If you feel your partner stiffening at any moment, use that stiffness to throw her off balance.

you

Snake Creeps Down

This posture suggests a snake creeping along the earth or in the water. Keep your body lowered so that your belly button is close to your knees. This is actually an escape movement. If you happen to face a real opponent (who may be a lot bigger than you), retreat can be a good idea. The purpose of a retreat is to be able to advance later with more success.

1 Begin in a lunge stance—with your left leg facing forward and your knee bent. The toes of your left foot should be pointed straight ahead. Stretch your right leg back, with your right knee slightly flexed.

2 Extend your left arm, keeping your elbow slightly flexed. Keep your hand and fingers in an open position.

3 Put your right arm back and to the right of your body. Point the fingers of your right hand toward the floor.

4 Keep your hands in the same general position throughout the movement.

5 Turn out your right foot so it's at a right angle to your right leg. Most of your weight should be on your left leg. Be careful to maintain your balance.

6 Shift your weight back onto your right foot. At the same time, lower your body closer to the floor.

7 Keep your back straight. If you lean forward, you will make your head a target, and it'll be easier to hit!

8 Don't let your right knee collapse inward. Keep your right foot turned out slightly to help maintain your balance.

White Crane Spreads Its Wings

This posture is also known as stork spreads its wings. It is an important posture in tai chi. It teaches you how to step to the side of your opponent and, if possible, behind her. In tai chi, you're constantly shifting your weight from leg to leg. You're never in one position for very long.

1 Stand with your feet parallel and shoulder-width apart and your knees bent slightly. Your arms should be by your sides.

2 Shift the majority of your weight to your left leg. At the same time, raise your left arm so it's parallel with your chest. Move your right arm down so it's slightly touching your right thigh.

3 Bend your right knee so that the toes of your foot lightly touch the floor to give you balance.

4 At the same time, pull your right hand down in front of your lower body.

5 Turn your body slightly to position your right shoulder forward. This is called the center position and is used as a transition between movements. The movements should be graceful and flowing.

6 Lift up your right foot, and place it back down in the same position. Don't shift your weight yet.

7 Shift your weight to your right foot, and start turning your body to the left.

8 Your left arm should start to swing down and your right arm should start to swing up, propelled by the turning of your waist. Don't change the level of your body when stepping or shifting your weight. As the weight shifts to your right foot, the left foot pivots on the toe to the left.

GLOSSARY

Aikido: A nonviolent Japanese martial art developed in the 1930s that uses flowing, circular movements to throw an opponent off balance.

Block: A move to stop an opponent from hitting your body.

Chi: The Chinese word for internal energy; spiritual and physical force generated through breathing techniques studied in martial arts. Chi can be traced to the gentle art of yoga. See also *ki*.

Dojo: A school or training hall where Japanese martial arts are practiced.

Form: A term for the precise pattern of moves that Japanese martial artists memorize and practice to demonstrate grace and agility. See also kata.

Gi: The white, loose-fitting uniform worn when practicing martial arts, especially karate.

Judo: A Japanese defensive art that teaches techniques involving throwing, grappling, and pressure points.

Jujitsu: A martial arts style first practiced in Japan centuries ago by samurai warriors. Students today learn punches, strikes, kicks, throws, locks, and grappling techniques.

Karate: A complex system of techniques that uses almost every part of the body to punch, strike, kick, or block.

Karateka: A person who practices karate.

Kata: Japanese for "form"; a series of choreographed movements students memorize to display their skills in karate.

Ki: The Japanese word for chi, or internal energy.

Kung fu: A general term for Chinese martial arts that loosely translates as "skill" or "work." Its several hundred styles are linked to nature and include movements made by the white crane, praying mantis, and monkey.

Ninja: A person trained in ninjitsu, the ancient Japanese martial art of stealth. Ninjas used to be involved with spying and assassinations.

Obi: Japanese for the belt used in martial arts training; different colors denote different skill levels.

Osu: "Hello," "Good-bye," "Yes, I understand." Said when bowing to the sensei, or instructor, in a Japanese martial arts class.

Samurai: Ancient Japanese warriors who were skilled in the arts as well as in many martial arts practices, especially the sword.

Sensei: "Teacher" in Japanese; a term used to address the instructor in a martial arts class. See also *sifu*.

Sifu: The Chinese term for "teacher." Used to address the instructor in a martial arts class.

Sparring: Martial arts training with a partner for sport without intentionally hurting the other person.

Tae kwon do: A popular Korean martial art developed in the 1950s. Known for its high kicks.

Tai chi chuan: Chinese martial art characterized by movements that are slow, continuous, circular, well-balanced, and rhythmic.

Yin-yang: The idea that the universe is made up of both conflict and harmony. Yin symbolizes the negative and destructive; yang symbolizes the positive and creative.

Yoga: A system of controlling the mind, body, and spirit through breathing, stretching, and exercise techniques.

INDEX

CREDITS

Alice Jablonsky, Author
In her quest for the perfect workout, Alice Jablonsky discovered martial arts 20 years ago. She first studied tang soo do, a Korean martial arts style. Since then, she has worked up a sweat doing kickboxing and has focused on the mind-body connection doing tai chi and yoga. Alice is the author of nearly a dozen books for young people, including *Discover Ocean Life* and *101 Questions about Desert Life*. Her other fun jobs have included writing and editing for *National Geographic*, Hasbro, and LeapFrog.

Shelly Meridith Delice, Illustrator
Shelly Meridith Delice grew up in a small farm town in Kansas. She now lives in a loft in New York City with her husband and daughter, Zinedine. She has been designing toys and illustrating books for 15 years.

Martial Arts Consultants

Morgan Newman
Morgan Newman manages instruction and training at Richard Lee's Five Star East-West Kung Fu & West Coast Headquarters School in Northern California. She holds a second-degree black belt in kung fu.

Jim Cale
Jim Cale has studied various martial arts, including karate, judo, and jujitsu for over a decade. He holds a black belt degree in jujitsu.

Jason Morris
Jason Morris is a Fourth Dan Black Belt International Instructor and Examiner with the International Taekwon-Do Federation.

Victoria Brovont
Victoria Brovont has been training in martial arts for the past 10 years. She has studied a wide variety of styles, including jujitsu, tae soo do, hwa rang do, and tae kwon do.